Socialism and Marriage
Aldred, Guy A.

ISBN: 978-1-387-92812-5

2022 Independent Publisher

Charleroi, PA USA

Socialism and Marriage

Guy A. Aldred

CONTENTS

Foreward

This pamphlet was published at Shepherds Bush in 1914. It was revised from *The Religion and Economics of Sex Oppression*, which was printed and published by the Bakunin Press, at the Goswell Road address in 1907. The purpose of the original pamphlet was described on the title page as follows:

> "Being a consideration of the principles of Socialism and Freethought in relation to Women, The Suffrage, Free Love, and Neo-Malthusian, together with an examination of scriptural precepts and injunctions, the teaching of the Christian Fathers, and of the Latter Day Saints upon the questions of polygamy and the position of woman."

The Foreword mentions how the pamphlet owed its inception to a lecture delivered before the Southwark Socialist Club (S.D.F.) on January 7th, 1906, on "Socialism and Woman." It concludes by dedicating "my present effort to my comrade, Rose Witcop." Subsequently, my relationship with Rose Witcop became an interesting legal question and gave rise to much newspaper comment. That relationship and the legal question merit discussion in a separate work. The original preface can be reproduced later.

The 1911 rewritten essay omitted the Mormon satire on Marriage Relations and sermon on Jesus as a polygamist. This ought not to have been deleted but should have been reviewed more thoroughly. A considerable section of the 1907 pamphlet that was deleted from the 1911 revision ought to have been removed to an appendix. In 1912 in the *Herald of Revolt*, and later, in *The Spur*, the author discussed at greater length the various aspects of the question of women's emancipation. It is my intention to bring all these essays together in another pamphlet.

The full (1907) reference to the Church Fathers and their views on woman has been restored in place of the more general summary published in the revised pamphlet.

Glasgow, May 9, 1940.

G. A. A.

Chapter 1

The Bible is not a divinely inspired book. Its every line is not sacred. Its very periods are not inspired. Its whole prospect is not awful. Penetrate the gloom with which the Christian centuries have surrounded the ancient "book above books," and you will discover nothing more than an old-time "book of books." In this literary miscellany, it is impossible to discover an even distribution of talent. The books are not equally good. Every passage is not expressive of a common level of ability on the part oi the authors. Many sentences challenge publication. As many merit oblivion. Outlooks, it has in abundance from that of Moses, gluttonous for power, to that of Isaiah, stern for the righteousness of liberty. Minor priests rub shoulders with minor prophets. Drama is found in job, cynical materialism in Ecclesiastes, and the championship of secular authority only in Saul. Pentateuchal polygamy is mingled with much divine imbecility. Sinai storms at sense. But the captivity is followed by denunciations of useless ritual and canting ceremony. The God with "back parts" gives place to the God of spirit; the jealous to the zealous deity. His holiness hungers not for sacrifice from the strong, but thirsts to sustain the weak. It abandons dominion to cast out oppression. Works recording so radical a transformation of the divine character or characters must boast a little genius in places. Suspicion of such cannot be avoided entirely.

Of this natural magazine of literature, or collection of writings, no mention will be made in this essay. We shall write only of a supernatural "books of books." This is a, circumspect "line in literature" which time has rendered acceptable to the kirk elder and the bethel deacon. Since it is treated to no variety of appreciation, it is discovered to possess no divergency of style, nor lights or shades of merit. It is the book. Not a fossil, but a whole geological stratum.

This is what the Hebrew literary museum has been hallowed into being by the Church, which has disciplined the intellect of man to stagnation. One day we shall understand the stratum so well that we shall discover not merely fossils but living forms—the living forms of past struggles for freedom. In the fetish, we shall glimpse the truth. At present, we can see nothing beyond a rod of authority, which narrows our vision, curbs our liberty, and commands our slavish devotion.

Mankind evolved and embraced this rod of authority in the ages when darkness was its only light. Rod and victim experienced a common degradation. Where all was divine equally, the vulgar was divine mostly. The power of the rod consisted in its rudeness. The subjection of the people lay in their lewdness. Wisdom was the flourish of accidence, which ornamented the ecclesiastical crook. The Bible itself was its most imbecile portions. Pearls were refuse because husks were gems. God's "blind mouths" secured social sanctuary, whilst power destroyed perspective, and interest nursed misery.

We are devout neither about nor towards this Bible of despotism. We dare not pretend a respect for the Bible of reality, for the Christian world knows of no reality outside of the Bible of pretense. Its worthlessness calls for exposure. We will discuss its relation towards w0man's freedom, because our social greatness, involving woman's subjection, is held to -be founded upon the said holy writ.

God's word treats woman not to a lesson, but to a dirge. It 'compliments our mothers and sisters by insisting on their vicious curiosity and ambition. Woman's inherently corrupt nature is presumed to corrupt all her male posterity. In the female line, there is so much spontaneous sin that no room remains for any inherited taint. Fatherhood is virtue, whilst motherhood is vice. It is unclean to suffer the pain of "presenting" one's masculine proprietor, called husband, with a child. It is clean to have been the cause of the presentation. But it is doubly unclean to bear a female instead of a male child. One wonders how the father 'escapes contamination in this event.

What the Jewish Code of Leviticus says in this connection, the Anglican Service for the Churching of Woman retains. Female hysteria applauds the lie.

God decreed that woman should be subject unto man. He destined her for child-bearing at her husband's will and domestic drudgery on his behalf. Obedience must be paid to his every whim, care given to his comforts, ministering to his passions, and submission to his castigation. The most exemplary attention to the servitude of this underpaid housekeeping is rewarded with pain and sorrow. From Eve to Dorcas, the records oi the duet woman 'characters in the Bible, preach the same dreary morality.

Even when exercising the virtue of most complete humility, woman remains an abomination. Even when exhibiting no initiative, she exerts an evil influence. Good dwelt in Nazareth, but it has never dwelt in woman.

Leah and Rachel were so much cattle given in wedlock to Jacob as a reward for seven years' service each. On the most flattering estimate they were but good wages. Maybe their lord and master often viewed them less charitably.

The Jewish Lord oi Hosts was a God of Rape. In Deuteronomy, he bade the Hebrews force beautiful captives from among their fallen enemies--unto whom they might have a desire—to be their wives. In judges, he has the sons of Benjamin waylay the daughters of Shihol.

Man was the human being. Woman was the female. She completed that sex nature, which was incidental to his physical "make-up. After Constantine, the Church Fathers, who relished sacred writ, gravely discovered that she had no soul, and noted, without alarm, that she died like a dog.

To this day, a similar dictum prevails. Man is mankind and woman is the sex. It is the function of man to dispose of her body, as his own dependence on the laws of brute force, fraud, and purchase decide. She has no right to object, no need to consent. Everything is done for her. Man proposes, man disposes, and the 'woman changes hands. What will be, will be.

When a man dies, his "relict" is permitted to survive. She continues his shadow until she completes another human being's ;sex. Instead of a relic, she is now an appendage.

In the Jewish ritual, she is permitted to discharge no functions requiring individual initiative In the framing of the creed, canons, and codes of Christendom her voice has never -been heard.

Jesus denied the God of Abraham and placed woman on terms of equality with her accusers. The heresiarchs——Cerdon, Carpocrates, and Paul of Samosata—applauded this view and repudiated Old Testament authority. Visiting them with excommunication, "the Church accepted 'Constantine and Jehovah, and treated the world to those councils, doctrines, relics, monastic institutions, and forgeries which have been the wonders of sixteen centuries.

It invented the story of the resurrection.

Thomas felt the wounds in Christ's side. Mary was not good enough to touch "the risen savior." Since he was man, an eternal soul, the testimony of Thomas counted. Since she was woman, the sex instrument of man, the evidence of Mary was of no moment. What she saw or heard could have no weight in the decision of the Church.

Much is made of the alleged fact, that Christianity has "honored" woman. Much, also, is said of the historical authenticity of the Christian Scriptures. In support of which authenticity, defenders of the saintly faith refer us to the Pagan Christian fathers.

Some of these fathers may be quoted in favor of Communism and they are not always completely heterodox. Did the faithful folk, who cite these worthies without question, believe in Jesus and understand the story of his teaching and its historic perversion and negation, they would be given less to this weakness. In the main, despite their varying degree of heresy, these gentlemen were mostly ecclesiastical time-servers. Each is the voice of the Church, not when he proclaims the truth of his particular heresy, but only in his appalling declaration of allegiance to superstition and oppression. The arrogance and ignorance has, oi these Church Fathers, combined to become the gospel of

Christendom. Some of them may have urged Communism. All opposed the freedom of woman, -denied her equity and justice in her relations with the male human.

St. Chrysostom describes woman as "a necessary evil, a natural temptation, a desirable calamity, a domestic peril, a deadly fascination, and a painted ill." Obviously, cosmetics, lipstick, sun-tan, rouge, are as ancient as the 'Church Fathers! The same saint. asserted that "through woman the Devil has triumphed, through her paradise has been lost; of all wild beasts, the most dangerous." Equally worthy of a Christian thinker, and similar in letter and in spirit to this sweetly sympathetic dictum is that of Tertullian, who addressed woman as "the Devil's gateway," and "unsealer of the forbidden tree," "the first deserter of the divine law," "who destroyed so easily God's image, man." Then there is the declaration of St. Gregory the Great, to the effect that "woman has the poison of the asp, and the malice of a dragon." St. Jerome, who invented the doctrine of heavenly salvation and substituted it for the doctrine of mental health, eulogized woman in his quaint style as "the gate of the devil, the road of iniquity, the dart of the scorpion." This vies, in strength of declaration, with the word picture created by the Christian genius of Clement of Alexandria. This noble soul denounces affection for a woman as leading "to the fire that will never cease in consequence of sin.'? Gregory Thaumaturgus placed it on record, that, "verily, a person may find one man chaste among a thousand, but a woman never." St. Bernard apostrophized her as "the organ of the Devil." St. john Damascene contented himself with the comparatively mild description: "the daughter of falsehood, a sentinel of Hell, the enemy of Peace," through whom "Adam lost his paradise."

Similar testimony is borne 'by St. Antony, Bonaventure and Cyprian, who regarded woman, respectively, as "the fountain of sin, the arm of the Devil, her voice the hissing of the serpent"; "the scorpion, ever ready to sting, the lance of the demon"; and "the instrument which the devil uses to gain possession of our souls."

This is "the good news" that woman has welcomed down the Christian centuries! For a thousand years, the insane and inane denunciation of woman has been the teaching of Christendom. Even when it was no longer as the gospel of Christian civilization, this teaching inspires secretly the approach to woman as something uncanny if not positively socially unclean in herself. The parade of gallantry 'conceals the real attitude. Whoever believes that the church fathers voice "the truth" of 'Christianity must accept the degradation of woman as a divine decree. Whoever regards the god oi Abraham as the heavenly pater of Jesus, must look upon polygamy as compatible with God's law. Holy writ boasts no express discharge against it, and the holy spirit often commends it.

Chapter 2

The dutifully pious young lady of to-day does not believe in polygamy. When she sells her chastity in the marriage market, she is guaranteed a legal monopoly. That satisfies her conscience. She does not inquire whether or not the man is offering her damaged goods. Indeed, she half suspects that he has sown wild oats in the company of other women. Henceforth, these are to have no claim on him. So her jealous sense of honor is satisfied.

Polygamy, though Biblically sanctioned, dishonors woman, by making her the property of man. It lays it down that one man has the right to own a number of women as his lawful wives, and have connection with others as his unlawful passions dictate. Under polygamy, the aim of every woman is to be a lawful wife if she would be counted "respectable."

Monogamy, though legally established, dishonors woman, by making her the property of man. It lays it down that one man has the right to own one woman as his lawful wife, and have connection with others as his unlawful passions dictate. Under monogamy, the aim of every woman is to be a lawful wife if she would be counted "respectable."

The position of the wife under both systems is the same. She purchases her position by her chastity. The chastity of the man is another matter. A wife cannot be divorced from her husband through his having committed adultery alone. There must be, in addition, the proven charges of cruelty and desertion. Should the wife commit adultery, the husband can obtain a divorce, and monetary damages against the corespondent, as a solatium for his injured feelings.

Woman is the property of man. In marriage, she has no name of her own, no right of parentage. Any man who, being unmarried to a woman, attempts to force caresses on her is penalized for assault. judge and jury have decided, however, that a husband is entitled to a show of his wife's affections. He has purchased that right, and may abuse her body, in consequence, for years.

Not a few atheists attack the Bible for its polygamous teachings, on the ground that they degrade woman. They denounce Mormonism for putting the teachings into practice, as a "horrible example" to other Christian systems.

Of course, they deny that marriage is a sacrament of the church. Today, after years of struggle, the State has been compelled to accept their view, that marriage is only a secular contract. What good has this "reformed outlook" done woman? In what way has it affected the hypocrisy of marriage?

Let no man, says the Church sacrament, put asunder those whom God hath joined together. In other words, let the Godfearing lawyers do it, if you are rich enough to pay them. Surely if God exists, it should be left to him to join the chosen ones together. Only blasphemy can expect the priest, who does not know God's will, to do it. Only impiety can dread, that, without an idle ceremony, God cannot join together those whom he wishes to have united.

The secular contract is as binding as the Church sacrament. It is as substantially dishonoring to woman. It is equally false. To. object to mentioning God's name in the ceremony, when you do not object to the slavish covenant it involves, is cant of the worst possible description. To demand secular instead of ecclesiastical marriage, when virtue demands the abolition of all marriage, is humbug. Marriage gave a Christian preacher the power to deprive Annie Besant of her children. Had she been unmarried, she would have owned both herself and her children. As it was she was his property, and her children belonged to him. It was not ecclesiastical marriage that did this, as distinct from secular marriage, but marriage-the legalized sex relationship. Yet Annie Besant, in an eloquent pamphlet on "Marriage: As it Was, As it Is, and As it Should Be," published in 1882, pleaded for a written contract between the parties to a marriage union.

Annie Besant urges marriage reform, and simple divorce on the grounds of incompatibility. Simple divorce is merely a legalized form of pure and simple mating in the terms of free love, for it is marriage and separation at will. Only the mating and separating are registered. This timid, incomplete, and hypocritical approach to the solution of the problem is the last hopeless gesture of property society. The need for divorce means that monogamy is no more satisfactory to mankind than polygamy. Actually, different mating systems should exist side by side in a sane and civilized society.

It is the woman's place to take care of the children. She must bear unwanted children, and care for them amid much misery. If she neglects this duty, she is sent to prison, and her children to the workhouse. Her husband can plead that he was not responsible for his wife's neglect. Woman suffers all the penalties of a parent. She enjoys none of the rights.

Under a promise oi marriage, a young woman consents to cohabit with the man to whom she has been engaged for a number of years. He fails to make good, and the victim of his lust becomes a social outcast at a moment when she needs most friendship. No one owns her or her offspring. Were there no marriage laws, such callous outrage would be impossible.

Dissenting cant views her as an "unfortunate." It is wrong. Moral conventionalism follows suit. It is wrong. The secular marriage has no meaning if it is not destined to serve the same end. It is as hypocritical as the ecclesiastical sacrament.

If woman did not lose her identity when she married, no one» could object to her bearing children in her own right. If she owned her body in marriage, there would be no shame attached to owning it out of marriage.

But if woman owned her body, the marriage profession would be gone. There would be no harlots to sell their bodies for a night. There would be no respectable women to sell their bodies for life. Children could not be la-belled bastards for a fictitious offense, and women would be betrayed no more. Rape would disappear, -both by contract, and without it.

Men and women would not commit adultery and practice desertion to escape a wedded prostitution that did not exist. Irrational promises would not -be terminated by unnecessary divorces. Papers would not carry notices of men and women's intentions to sleep together. They would not announce the abandonment of the practice, or record reasons for changing partners.

Women's boast of marriage respectability is man's exhibition of his dishonor. It the father, son, husband, and sweetheart, did not outrage some women, other women would not be able to avow their honorable unions. Marriage bribes some women and degrades others, that man may parade his sex infamy.

Human nature is shamed and dishonored not by this or that ceremony of marriage. It is outraged by the institution itself. The moral of well-being of mankind demands the abolition of marriage. Woman must own her own body. She must choose the father or fathers of her children. If name they must have, that name should be hers. Only this means not reform but revolution.

Chapter 3

"Marriage," wrote the late Dr. E. P. McLoghlin, "is not an empty form; it is an indissoluble, untruthful, and unfounded contract, terminable only by death or dishonor. Untruthful and unfounded because the contractor saith, 'I will love.' He cannot do this; to love is beyond the power or domain of will. He may say, 'I do love.' But 'I will love,' he cannot and ought not to say. 'The law which would make her his.' I neither acknowledge the righteousness, nor even the possibility of any law save that of mutual consent——that is, affection. I do not desire to make any woman mine; it must be her love for me, and my love for her, which alone can dictate an inviolable relationship between us. In the presence of that love, either soluble or indissoluble bond, other than the influence of that love, is as insulting as it is necessary; in the absence of that love, any bond is as untruthful and useless as it is immoral."

The foregoing argument is unanswerable. Whenever it or any similar line oi reasoning is advanced, no one attempts to reply to it. Every defender of the legal institution will admit its validity, and then proceed to question its morality.

First, do we believe that one man should possess a woman or that she should be common property? This is supposed to bring the blush of shame to the cheek, and expression of horror to the eyes. A little calm reflection will dispose of it.

We have not proposed that woman should be common property. That is polyandry. Under polyandry, a woman no more owns her body than under polygamy or monogamy. All three systems decline to entertain the notion that woman should dispose of her own body as she thinks fit. In every case, it is the man's not the woman's desire, which counts. The woman may desire to have connection with only one man, with no man at all, or with several men at different times. That is her own affair. We propose that she should dispose of her body accordingly. To no man would belong the privilege of invading this right. How then can one talk of no ownership but self-ownership being collective ownership?

Next it will be urged that this involves promiscuity. But does not the. division of woman into two camps—"respectable" and otherwise—argue the. existence of promiscuity? It promiscuity does not degrade man to-day, why should it degrade woman tomorrow? At least, it would be an honest promiscuity, and woman could select a healthy parent for her child. Since the free woman could never be run to the marriage cover, her body could never be outraged or her person degraded.

Having urged that freedom involves promiscuity, the defender of legal marriage takes a lofty attitude. Promiscuity would degrade human' nature. Maybe; but if human nature is above promiscuity, how could freedom reduce it to this condition? If monogamy is the result of personal dignity, and cultured feeling, freedom can give only full and free expression to that dignity and feeling. Then only those alliances not based on either dignity or culture will disappear in a state of freedom. If the woman lives with a man because she loves him, not because she is tied to him, given freedom to decide, her choice will be unaffected. Wherein, then, is it wrong for a woman to own her body not up to the time she sleeps with a certain sex-mate, but for all time?

Let us canvass, fully, the significance of this word, "promiscuity." Annie Besant, pleading for monogamy, has pointed out, how, in the lower ranges of animal life, difference of sex is enough to excite passion. Here there is no individuality of choice. Among savages, this is negated. It is still the female that is loved, but individual beauty decides the connection. We rise to the civilized man; and find that he needs, in addition to sex difference, and beauty of form, completion of his higher nature. He needs satisfaction for heart, mind, and tastes.

From this it is argued that, the more civilized the nature, the more durable does the marriage relationship become. It may easily prove otherwise. The exclusive marriage union is a standard set up by the prudery which objects to mixed 'bathing and a pre-nuptial knowledge of sex physiology. It implies that the joy of sex can never be known unless, in every instance, it results in a certain act. Behind this view, is the idea of the hunter, of courtship, of the slavery of woman. As men and women mix more freely, as the charm of health and the lights and shades of character express

themselves more variously, in wider and wider circles of social intercourse, it does not follow that monogamy will disappear entirely. But it does follow that the prime consideration will he healthy minds and healthy bodies, joy, laughter, romping children, and social service.

That a man has been father of one woman's child, is no reason why, if his character completes that of another woman, he should not 'be father of her child. It will not affect the pain of bearing the child, or the pleasure of caring for him.

"What about the children?" asks the moralist of to-day. Well, what about them? Is the child's right to live to turn upon the fact that he needs food, clothing, shelter, and attention? Or, is it to be decided by the fact that his father had had sex connection with but one woman? Where consideration of the children is supreme, the moral code of the parents does not matter. But if the question is the legality of some birth over others, it is sheer cant to talk about the children. Nature never created bastards. It was social respectability and prurient prudery.

That the matter has an economic aspect we are aware. Its discussion will destroy the moral pretensions of the upholders of marriage, and bring us clown to the materialistic factor. We shall discover then that injustices attributed to free love, are common to class society. Marriage will be revealed as a vice, reflecting vicious economic circumstances.

Chapter 4

"That a man and woman should occupy the same house, and daily enjoy each other's company——so long as such an association gives birth to virtuous feelings, to kindness, to mutual forbearance, to courtesy, to disinterested affection—I consider right and proper," wrote Robert Dale Owen in the Barton Trumpet, in May, 1831. "That they should continue to inhabit the same house and to meet. daily, in case such intercourse should give birth to vicious feelings, to dislike, to ill-temper, to scolding, to carelessness of each other's comfort, and a want of respect for each other's feelings—this, I consider, when the two individuals alone are concerned, neither right nor proper; neither conducive to good order nor virtue. I do not think it well, therefore, to promise, at all hazards to live together for life."

Most persons will agree with the above plea for divorce. It asserts the immorality of the marriage tie. It puts all contracts out of the question. Once the right to disregard laws in the part is admitted, the duty of ignoring them in their entirety is implied. And every fresh concession made in the direction of rendering divorce easier—for the wealthy, and not for the poor, however—is a confession of the failure morally of the laws to secure that harmony of being they are presumed to effect. For laws are but the perpetuation of past errors. To realize this tact is to believe in divorce. To subscribe to divorce is to accept free love. If tree love involves promiscuity, divorce involves it. The issue is between anarchy in love and compulsory loveless connection.

"When the two individuals alone are concerned," qualifies R. D. Owen. Can any sane person believe that it is either right or proper, either conducive to good order or virtue on the part of the children to be brought up in a loveless home? Do not the children learn to hate their parents, and leave home at the earliest possible date in consequence?

Family life is the great lie of civilization. Parents sacrifice their honor for their children, and children destroy their genius for their parents.

What of the children? Are there no foundling hospitals? Are there no mothers denied the right to bring their children up tenderly, because they, the mothers, were not wedded to the fathers? What of these children?

Since when has God told man it was justice to oppress the weak? If the foundling home is good enough for some children, it is good enough for all.

Under free love, all men would desert their children. Of course the argument is nonsense. Nothing of the kind would take place. All men are not scoundrels. Admitting that the present financial system continued, and that all fathers deserted the children, woman would cease to be the household drudge, man would become his own domestic serf, and the children, at the worst, would become all foundlings. They would -be clothed and fed, as to-day they are educated, by the state or else the community. If they are not pauperized by receiving common free education, they will not he pauperized by receiving common free clothing and food. If they are, then illegitimates should not be pauperized in this way. 'The marriage laws should go, in the interest of the illegitimate.

This would have an economic effect. The workers' wages are governed -by his cost of production. When the luxury of family life ceased to enter into that cost, his wages would decline. The children, heirs of the commonwealth, would be kept still out of the workers' labor power.

We have said the question is an economic one. It is. No man has the right to help a woman because she needs help. If she has children by another man, however great her suffering, his chivalry must not lend a helping hand. Only where he has assaulted the woman's chastity is he permitted to assist her. It is not justice, not the sufferings of the woman, not the tears of the children. It is the owning of the w0man's person that counts. Men who believe in marriage laws laugh at the idea of "keeping" another man's children. Why? Does the worker not keep the children of the rich-—and the parents into the bargain?

Analyze it, and this family life plea becomes individualism run mad. Driven by the wants of his family, the dock-worker fights for his job. Does he care about the family life of the weaker man he has ousted? Hunger and misery evolve a thief. The need to live manufactures the detective. Both have families. Both fight for them. The limb of the law wins—and his family is happy. The thief loses—-and a family tragedy is enacted. What of the children? Does the wedding-ring give them food?

"When the Scottish miners came out on strike in 1894," wrote Mr. Chisholm Robertson recently in the Glasgow Evening Times, "and throughout the strike the miners of England and Wales continued at work, filled the markets depleted by the abstention from work of the Scottish miners. This was a veritable harvest to the miners over the border. It prolonged, however, the fight, finally defeating it, with much suffering to the families of the men on strike, great hardship to the workers of kindred trades, and entailed years of hurt to the Scottish coal trade."

The English miners were thinking of their wives and children. Their family considerations prevented them being just to all women and children of their class in whom they had no property. Good husbands can make poor citizens. Good fathers make poor fighters against class injustice. Surely the marriage which reduces a man to a scab should go. Surely we are less than brutes if we cannot realize that our lives are mean and narrow if we do not secure happiness and joy to others. When we realize that, the class-struggle is substituted for the family struggle. We are no longer husbands, wives, and children—but comrades and chums, freely associating as the propaganda and our interest in it demands.

Chapter 5

Mother Grundy believes that the two sexes cannot smile, without contemplating the sex-act. That a pleasant day cannot be spent without a similar consequence. That mixed bathing leads to suggestion. That a handclasp is fatal, and, even in moments either of extreme sorrow or extreme joy, the most humble kiss of sympathy is dangerous. At one time, no man was allowed to speak to a woman unless he had "honorable intentions." Properly translated, this meant dishonorable ones.

This is changed now, and Mother Grundy is wrong. The function of woman is not to share barracks with man, and bear him children. She is entitled to get all the health out of life possible. Free association gives that health; and as we mix no longer in the presence of a sex mystery, but understanding each other's physiology, sex may give charm to our friendship. It does not rush us into sex-connection. Knowing our freedom, we are lured on by no forbidden fruit, and only at supreme moments of passion will intercourse result.

We are speaking of Socialism, not of

Capitalism, where intercourse is a daily habit. Whilst full freedom belongs to Socialism, it would be wrong not to embrace its teachings and endeavor to live up to some of them to-day. To do so, is to break fundamentally with class-society; and even though we enter upon free marriage rather than into free-love relationships, it is but a step to the other, and prepares the philistine imagination for the dawn of matriarchal society.

In free marriage, both parties retain their identities. But the man, feeling bound by honor and duty, should his love cool, hesitates to avow the fact. Woman, owing to her inherited position in slave society, when emancipated even, too often experiences a jealousy which the free man does not experience. But his regard for his friend, and the children, if any, fetters his expression of his feelings. This is wrong—and must go. T-he ecclesiastical marriage, the secular marriage, and the

Chapter 6

Free love is impossible under capitalism. Yes: so is honor or truth of any description. Is that any reason why we should ask the priest to bless our sex-relationship, or the law to license our associations?

Woman is now a wage-earner. She suffers all the misery of free labor. She -bears all the chains of the past. Reduces her male colleague's wages by competition, and then maintains his existence on the lesser income. Legally, she remains his inferior.

In order to remove these anomalies, some middle—class women have been urging on the State their right to vote, and thus assist in the making of the laws that govern them. Superficially, the claim is incontrovertible. There is no reason why woman should not enjoy the same social rights as man. If men boast a property franchise, so should women. If a small set of male parasites vote, not according to their intelligence, but in ratio to the houses they own, logically a select clique of female parasites should be entitled to the same privileges. If a man can sit in the House of Pretense, woman can also. The sexes are equal in honor and dishonor. The property male vote is not the enfranchisement of men.

The limited equal enfranchisement of women is not suffrage for women. To pretend so, is ridiculous. Short of out and out adult suffrage, women suffrage is impossible.

Whilst one is securing the part, one can be realizing the whole. It is as easy to win "adult suffrage" as its palliative, "woman suffrage." The more loudly you demand the former, the more likely you are to secure the latter.

Adult suffrage, in its turn, is only a palliation——the shadow of political power which will be granted, one day, to prevent the surrender of the substance of economic power. There is a futility in striving for anything short of Socialism; and the suffrage struggle embodies that futility.

So long as the workers are dominated by the capitalist class, so long as they remain the economic slaves of society, so long will they lack that industrial liberty, without which all suffrage is a.. farce. Economic determinism, the slow but sure awakening of the masses to their real position, are the factors governing the nature of capitalistic concession; so that the nearer the people come to the realization of their condition, the more advanced will be the nature of the palliatives we shall secure, Hence there is no necessity to concentrate our energies upon the securing of palliatives. Let us come out for Socialism, and as the Bible has it, "these other things shall he added unto us." As with the limited franchise, so with adult franchise, both are equally absurd without economic conditions prevail that guarantee freedom from want, and are equally fraudulent, therefore, as battle-cries.

Free-love propaganda, if not discussed in the terms of its economic basis, may become an Utopian cause. Anti-State activity may prove the same. So may Atheist agitation. But free love is not a palliative. It is an expression of our Socialism, an avowal of our revolt. Anarchism is not a palliative. It either compromises to "direct action" and reforms itself into an abstraction, or remains revolutionary —— a statement of what Socialism politically and socially involves. Atheism is not a palliative Either it degenerates into a lifeless superstition of unreasoning reason, or just summarizes. the materialism of Socialism.

Socialism, then does not believe in votes under capitalism, petitioning to administer the capitalist system, either for men or women. It urges social freedom for both instead—a new economic order of living, social and industrial democracy.

These facts are commended to the attention of those who desire to hasten the dawn of the day when woman shall stand forth freed from the fetters of theological superstition and economic bondage. Let them but—

"See the blasting, burning shame of sex-oppression now,

And with hearts and hands uplifted, swear a grand and God-like vow,

That despite the fangs of custom, and despite the Church's frown,

Womanhood shall wield its scepter, womanhood shall wear its crown.

She hath borne with man his crosses, she has worn with him his chains,"

She hath shared in all his losses, she hath suffered all his pains.

She shall stand with him coequal, on
the pure-exalted plains."

Author's Note

In the 1907 pamphlet, the piety theme is developed in detail. The women characters of the Bible are listed by name and comment made, that their several stories "are included in the hope of inculcating in the woman's mind the propriety of her 'modest' (!) retirement to the privacy of domestic life, performing, in an exemplary manner, the duties of a domestic serf, studying his desires like a subject, whilst extolling him for his strength of mind, and power of acquiring knowledge and enforcing his will. To these disgusting precepts, We find even the boasted savior of Christendom made, by priestly tradition, to lend his aid."

This passage stands: but it would interfere with the re-written text of the 1914 edition to restore it to its place in the main essay.